SURVIVAL HISTORY

by John McClelland and Henderson Editors
Illustrated by Peter Rutherford

HENDERSON
PUBLISHING PLC

©1995 HENDERSON PUBLISHING PLC

FANTASTIC FOSSILS

This Survive at School guide is all you will need to enjoy history at school, so throw away those boring text books and get rid of your teacher by turning them into a fossil - most history teachers are living fossils anyway!

Just follow this step-by-step guide:

1 Remove all the flesh from their bones. (The chemistry teacher might help with this.)

2 Bury the skeleton in the school sandpit with some mud and a few rotting plants (see the school gardener).

3 Pile huge quantities of stones on top of the buried bones (borrow from geology department).

4 Leave to mature for a couple of million years.

5 Dig up and 'discover' your very own fossil teacher - you can keep them in the classroom as a special exhibit.

FOSSILIZED TEACHER 1990'S

Fossils are a very important part of history because they prove that the Earth was once ruled by primitive creatures called dinosaurs who did not invent the motorcar...

DUMB DATES

Now that the little matter of your teacher is sorted out, you can begin to enjoy history instead of having to learn endless lists of boring dates and useless facts about ancient battles.

Of course, some dates are important - especially the ones that grow on palm trees because they are delicious; all other dates divide into two types...

B.C. - this means Before Cricket and refers to any date before some time around 1550, when the game was invented.

A.D. - this means After Dwarfs and refers to any time after these little chaps became extinct in about 1603.

The time in between these dates is known as After Before Cricket Dwarfs or A.B.C.D. for short!

Some important dates to remember:

0 B.C. - absolutely nothing happens.

B.C. - world invaded by dinosaurs, fossils, insects, little green men from the planet Quork and Romans.

Shortly Afterwards - the little green men and the dinosaurs leave together to discover new worlds and go where no dinosaur has gone before.

1492 - Christopher Columbus discovers Disney World.

1969 - Neil Armstrong proves the moon isn't made of cheese after all.

SORRY GIRLS!

A quick note for all girl readers - as I am sure you will have noticed most history, especially the older sort, completely ignores girls.

This is because they were meant to sit at home combing their hair, knitting socks and doing a bit of embroidery or tapestry while the men ran around making history (and a nuisance of themselves).

Of course, there were some terrific exceptions:

Queen Boadicea was a kind of original Hell's Angel, but instead of charging around on her chopper terrorising old age pensioners, she rode around on a two-horsepower chariot terrorising Romans.

Queen Elizabeth I liked choppers, too - but mostly for cutting people's heads off. She wasn't very fond of the Spanish - when they came to Britain for their holidays, she ordered that all their boats be sunk before they could land. (See entry for Spanish Armada.)

Queen Victoria is famous for saying 'We are not amused'. This is because she had no sense of humour, which is understandable as she had 37 great-grandchildren and that means an awful lot of birthday presents!

There are other famous girls, of course... but we've, er, forgotten their names!

DOPEY DINOSAURS

Long before there were any people, the Earth was populated by dinosaurs - imagine that?

No drive-in burger bars,
no motorway tailbacks,
no television,
no package holidays,
no nuclear power stations,
no nothing...

NOT EVEN SCHOOL!

- well, all right, the last bit sounds okay - but can you imagine living in a world without all these marvellous human inventions? - of course you can't!

That's why dinosaurs are extinct; they died of boredom...or at least almost all of them did...

One particularly stupid specimen called *Dopeysaurus Maximus* paddled across the English Channel from France and was the first creature to discover England. It was going to plant a little flag and make a speech when it forgot why it was there (very small brain), so it wandered north and eventually fell into a big loch in Scotland where it still is today - can you guess the name of the loch?

Some smarty-pants scientists think that crocodiles are a modern-day dinosaur, but this is nonsense as they were invented, quite recently, by the leather industry for making handbags and expensive shoes. (Not nice!)

STONE THE CROWS

Now we are getting to the interesting bits where human beings first appear in the world and start changing things.

The first humans seem to have arrived about 70,000 years ago - so if you meet one, offer them a chair and a cup of tea as they are going to be a bit old and doddery.

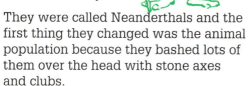

They were called Neanderthals and the first thing they changed was the animal population because they bashed lots of them over the head with stone axes and clubs.

Now you know where the phrase 'Stone The Crows' comes from, though it could just as easily have been 'Stone The Rabbits' or 'Look out lads, it's a sabre-toothed tiger!'.

These were Stone Age people because they made all their tools out of stone.

They were followed by the Bronze Age people who made all their tools out of bronze... and the Iron Age people who made all their tools out of irons - and very funny shapes they were, too!

Today, we would be called the D.I.Y. Superstore Age people because we get all our tools from great big warehouses.

POTTY PYRAMIDS

According to official history books, the Ancient Egyptians were one of the first great civilisations of the world - this is because they had invented the following:

The Pyramid

It took 40,000 workers 20 years to build one of these, so you had to order one well in advance if you wanted to be buried in it. Needless to say, they didn't catch on with other ancient civilisations because they had better things to do with their time - like inventing ice cream.

Mummies

These are big bundles of bandages shaped like human beings that wander about on dark nights scaring people. They were probably invented for Ancient Egyptian horror movies - trouble is, they forgot to invent the movie camera to film them with!

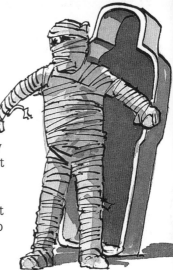

The Skinhead

Most Ancient Egyptians shaved their heads so they could look really mean and dangerous - they probably went to Ancient Egyptian football matches on Saturday afternoons and threw papyrus toilet rolls from the terraces!

TRAGIC GREEKS

The Ancient Greeks were a funny lot...

They liked performing plays but women were not allowed to take part (sorry girls) so men had to dress up for the female roles. Plays were either tragedies (really serious with lots of blood and guts and chopped-off heads), or comedies - mostly making fun of politicians, so nothing much has changed there.

The Ancient Greeks were also a sneaky lot...

Having tried to get into the city of Troy for ten years without success, they left a great big wooden horse outside the gates and retreated. The Trojans were so thick they actually wheeled the horse into their city. Surprise, surprise - that night, a pile of Greek soldiers who had been hiding inside it jumped out, opened the gates and 'Bob's Your Uncle'; no more Trojans.

The Ancient Greeks were a sporty lot, too...

Next time you're tortured half to death in the school gym or made to gallop round the athletics track, blame the Greeks. Being a tough bunch, they exercised regularly in sports centres, called Gymnasia, and held sports festivals, the most famous of which took place every four years in the city of Olympia...and that's where the Olympics come from.

ROAMIN' ROMANS

When they weren't feeding Christians to the lions or watching gladiators chop each other into little bits for fun, the Romans did a lot of travelling.

When they arrived in a foreign country they defeated the local army, made everybody into slaves, built a few roads and then constructed some Roman baths and spent most of their time soaking in hot water - very strange!

The Romans also enjoyed games, chariot races and food - fancy some larks' tongues and wild boar sausages?

Unfortunately, most Roman Emperors were completely mad:

- **Nero** set fire to Rome then watched it burn whilst playing a merry tune on his fiddle.

- **Caligula** fell in love with a horse and promoted it to a senior rank in the Senate, which is a Roman version of the Houses of Parliament - he probably called it the Horses of Parliament!

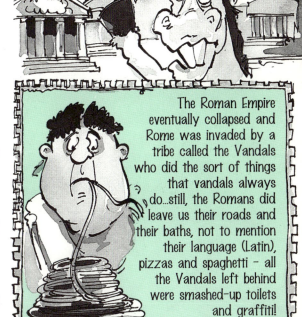

The Roman Empire eventually collapsed and Rome was invaded by a tribe called the Vandals who did the sort of things that vandals always do...still, the Romans did leave us their roads and their baths, not to mention their language (Latin), pizzas and spaghetti - all the Vandals left behind were smashed-up toilets and graffiti!

FABULOUS FIRSTS

Some carefully selected and very important facts to help you pass those horrible history tests...

- The first garden gnome was made in the Roman city of Pompeii about 2,000 years ago and is still dangling his little fishing rod into a pond to this day.

- The first fire engine was designed by a chap called Hero in the city of Alexandria 3,000 years ago - and what a hero he must have been!

- The first false teeth were supplied and fitted by Etruscan dentists 2,700 years ago - your dad's probably wearing a pair.

- Stonehenge was the first attempt at making a sun dial as it is aligned with the midsummer sunset and midwinter moonset. To read the time you would have had to fly over it in a helicopter, which is a pity because Stone Age helicopters were too heavy to fly!

- The first marathon runner was a bloke called Pheidippides who ran 42km non-stop with news of a military victory and dropped dead immediately afterwards - who said exercise was good for you?

VICIOUS VIKINGS

Vikings first appeared on the scene about 1,200 years ago. They sailed all over the place in their longships and are thought to have discovered America about 400 years before anyone else (see entry for America).

Unfortunately, Vikings seem to have been very bad-tempered and liked nothing better than beating up innocent bystanders, robbing churches and generally terrorising everyone - a bit like school bullies.

On the other hand, it must have been good fun being a Viking because everybody else was afraid of you and you could do whatever you wanted - they spent most of their time either fighting or throwing parties for their friends and generally having a good time.

If you were attacked by these axe-wielding madmen you could either run away, pretend to be a tree, hand over your pocket money or call them a bunch of big sissies and challenge them to a fight behind the bicycle sheds -

we do not recommend the last option!

STORMIN' NORMANS

The Normans came from France. They had names like Norman De Camembert, Norman De Roquefort, Norman De Brie and Norman De Wensleydale and were married to ladies called Norma.

In 1066, Harold, King of England, challenged all these Normans to a conker fight - this was a really stupid thing to do because the Norman leader was a nasty piece of work called William The Conker who had the best horse chestnut in Europe.

In the famous Battle of Hastings, William The Conker cheated by bashing Harold in the eye with his champion conker. Harold ran away and William became the new King.

From then on all the people of England had to be called Norman. They were not allowed to pick their own horse chestnuts in case anyone found a better one than William's.

The Normans took over all the horse chestnut forests and ordered loads of castles to be built by Motte and Bailey Ltd., castle builders by Royal Appointment.

If you meet someone today who is called Norman, do not challenge them to a conker fight - you have been warned!

MEDIEVAL MUCK

The Medieval period is the smelliest period of European history - no one ever washed, everything was infested by rats, fleas and mice and the contents of your toilet were just thrown out onto the street.

Because of this, almost everyone in Europe wanted to escape to somewhere less smelly, thus, some clever people invented the idea of the Crusades.

Basically, the Crusades were an excuse for all the smelly people in Europe to invade the area known as the Holy Land, a land full of holes which would have been very useful for dumping all their smelly rubbish in.

The people who lived in the Holy Land did not like this idea - hardly surprising - and their leader told all the smelly people to clear off back to where they came from.

The local sultan's name was Saladin and he was famous for inventing the green salad, Waldorf salad and blue cheese salad, amongst others.

To cut a long story short, the Crusades were not a success and the smelly Europeans were forced to go home and get their act together. The whole of Europe was given a good spring cleaning - this was called the Renaissance - and the people of the Holy Land gave them gallons of perfume, acres of carpet and lots of pre-packed salads as a bribe to stop them ever coming back again!

STRANGELY TRUE

Another collection of marvellous facts to bamboozle your history teacher with...

▪ **The first modern toilet** was invented by Thomas Crapper in the 1800's who was so flushed by his success that he went round the bend!

▪ **The largest single dish** in the history of the world is roasted camel prepared for Bedouin wedding feasts - cooked eggs are stuffed in fish, the fish stuffed in chickens, the chickens stuffed in a roasted sheep and the sheep stuffed into a whole camel - quite enough to give anyone the hump!

▪ **The first trousers for women** were designed by Amelia Bloomer in 1853 - blooming marvellous they were, too!

- **The first passenger train service** in the world opened in Kent in 1830. The steam engine pulled the train at 20k.p.h. and was called Stephenson's Rocket because it went so fast!

- **The largest sewage works** in the world opened in Chicago, U.S.A., in 1940 and treats 735,000,000 gallons of waste per day - Thomas Crapper would have been proud of it!

- **The oldest tinned food** in the world is roast beef canned by Donkin, Hall and Gamble in 1823. It was opened in 1958 which means it was one hundred and twenty-two years past its sell by date - pooh!

HERE, THERE AND EVERYWHERE

There was a time around the 13th and 15th centuries when big-headed numbskulls in Europe thought they were the smartest and most advanced people in the world - how wrong they were!

Here, there and everywhere were civilisations that were older and more advanced than anything in Europe:

- The Incas of Peru were fond of sun worship and guinea pigs - they invented factor 8 sun block and guinea pig kebabs.

- In Asia, the Mongols were led by Ghenghis Khan who was the most feared man in the world and inspired the famous song 'Anything you can do, Ghenghis Khan do better'.

- The Chinese were so shy that they invented the Great Wall of China to stop people staring at them.

- The Persians invented the flying carpet but Ali Baba and his forty thieves stole it.

- Indians invented the Indian rope trick, but when they climbed up the rope, they kept disappearing.

- Africans got along quite happily for thousands of years until the white men came. Many of these white men were from Holland and were called Boers because they talked so much they bored people to death. They made a country for themselves called the Orange Free State where no one was allowed to grow oranges - there's been trouble ever since.

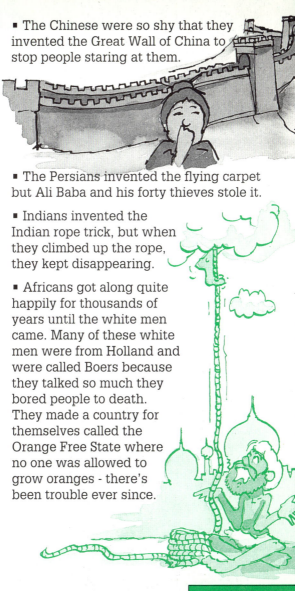

ELIZABETH THE WORST

Elizabeth the First, Queen of England from 1558-1603, didn't have the best of starts in life; her mother, Anne Boleyn, was executed by her father, Henry VIII, for treason. Then she was locked up in the Tower of London. Then her half-sister, Mary Queen of Scots, tried to have her assassinated.

Instead, Elizabeth had Mary's head chopped off after *she* had been crowned Queen, and things got better after that - they could hardly have got any worse, could they?

In fact, Elizabeth is supposed to have been a better ruler than most of the kings before her - that's girls for you!

She had two favourite knights...

Sir Walter Raleigh, who sailed to America and brought back potatoes and tobacco. In those days, they probably smoked the potatoes and served the tobacco mashed with butter and salt!

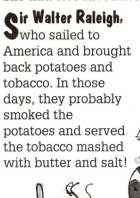

Sir Francis Drake, who was a bit of a pirate and liked nothing better than looting other people's ships to fill up the Royal Piggy Bank.

THE SPANISH ARMADA

There is a lot of nonsense talked about the Spanish Armada but the whole thing is quite easily explained...

In 1588, a group of fun-loving Spaniards decided it would be nice to visit England - heaven knows why as England was cold and wet, the food horrible and hotel accommodation of a very poor standard.

Probably because she didn't want the world to discover just how bad tourist facilities were in England, Elizabeth ordered British Immigration officials under the command of Sir Francis Drake, Lord Howard of Effingham and a few others to set sail, meet up with the Spaniards and persuade them to go home - after all, they had warm sunny weather and all-night discos, so what was the point of visiting England?

Unfortunately, there seems to have been some kind of disagreement and both sides started chucking insults and cannonballs at each other.

The rest is history, as they say; the Spanish ships were either sunk by gunfire or lost in heavy storms that blew up in the English Channel, and the tourists never did get a chance to enjoy good old-fashioned English hospitality.

Ever since, we Brits been visiting Spain for our holidays, instead...

OLIVER CRUMBLE

For a long time people thought the world was flat and that you could fall off the edge of it - these people were called Flatheads. Then some people decided the world was round, so they became known as Roundheads.

The Roundheads later started the English Civil War because Charles I, King of England, disagreed with them...

The leader of the Roundheads was Oliver Crumble who invented rhubarb crumble and the House of Commons - he thought there shouldn't be a king and that the country should be run by ordinary people...as long as their name was Oliver Crumble.

Charles I invented the King Charles Spaniel and not much else. He was a bit of a wimp as kings go and was always losing his head in a crisis.

The Roundheads won and King Charles lost his head for good on a chopping block.

However, the ordinary people soon got fed up eating rhubarb crumble and being told what to do. They decided it would be nice to have a new king and called him Charles II because that comes after Charles I - not very original but anyone called King Nigel or King Basil wouldn't have lasted very long now, would they?

YANKEE DOODLE CANDY

Just about *everybody* claims to have discovered America including Viking warriors, Irish monks and Christopher Columbus (did you know that poor old Columbus actually set sail to find India and landed in America by mistake? - I mean, they're only in opposite directions!).

In fact, America was not 'discovered' by any of these people since it hadn't been lost in the first place and all the native American tribes who lived there knew exactly where to find it.

In no time at all, the Indians had been pushed to one side and those smelly Europeans were at it again - remember the Crusades?

This time they landed in New York and headed west so they could chill out on the Californian beaches, invent the skateboard, the candy bar, Disneyland and Hollywood.

The most famous Americans are...

- General George Custard
- Wild Bill Hiccup
- George Washingline
- Henry Bored
- Franklin D. Roosterfelt
- Al Dogbone
- Silly The Kid
- Ernest Lemmingway
- Marylebone Munro
- Dr. Martin Luther Ping
- Roseanne Barr

...and Mickey Mouse and Donald Duck.

- they might have been better leaving it to the Indians!

VILE VICTORIANS

Victoria was Queen from 1837-1901 and many people think that the Victorian Age was one of the great ages of the world - maybe it was, but not for children. It's a horrible fact that the vile Victorians introduced compulsory schooling for the very first time...yes, it is hard to believe that they could have been so cruel!

Unless your parents were stinking rich or you were called little Lord or Lady Muckmasher, no one cared if you could read, write or count up to ten until the Victorians came along. Instead, you were likely to be given a nice job as a chimney sweep's brush or a farmer's scarecrow or sold into slavery to work in a big house washing posh people's knickers twenty-four hours a day.

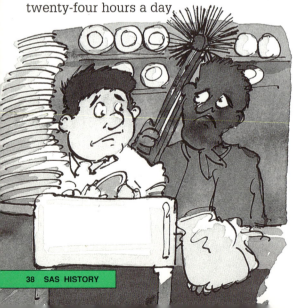

Then a lot of do-goody Victorians changed all that; no more enjoying yourself begging or digging turnips for wages of two pence a year - now you had to go to rotten school and be taught the three R's (wriggling, writhing and restlessness) by a horrible bully with a cane and a bad temper.

Even if you ran away to begin a career as a pickpocket or burglar's apprentice, they wouldn't leave you alone - the Victorians started the first police force (called Peelers), who liked nothing better than catching runaway children and returning them to the classroom - cruel times indeed!

A STICKY END

History is full of gruesome stories. As if things weren't bad enough, what with the plague, great fires, dirty water and no microwaves, other perils were invented to keep honest folk quaking in their sackcloth!

Like punishment. The stocks were a great source of entertainment in medieval Britain and Europe (not for the poor fellow locked inside them). All the neighbours gathered on the village green to hurl cabbages or rotting manure at the culprit. Even nagging wives were sometimes put into stocks.

Thieves copped much worse treatment. Many had a finger, an ear or even a hand chopped off, to mark them forever.

Much more fun was the ducking stool ... for the on-lookers, that is. The chair was mounted on a see-saw, and plunged into the village stream, 'til the unfortunate victim squealed ... or half-drowned.

In the Tower of London, beheading was all the rage. *Off with her head!* yelled the King one day when he was bored with his poor wife. *Off with his head!* yelled the King's parliament. Oh, happy days.

Then the French came up with a *trés chic* method. Voilà the guillotine. So clean, so quick - and the head plops neatly into a basket, boasts Monsieur Guillotine. Just ask Madam Marie Antoinette. Ooh, là là, non, per'aps not.

Into the 19th century with a bang... or rather, bang, bang, bang, bang! Desperados could join the friendly Foreign Legion, but when the sand, the dust and the scorpions got too much and they decided to run away (across the desert - called deserting!) the French came up trumps again - with the firing squad!

So how about a voyage to sunny Australia, or South America? All you had to do was steal a loaf of bread ... trouble was, it was no holiday camp. You were shipped, in chains, to some remote insect-ridden swamp called a penal colony, never to return.

R.I.P.

WHO SAID THAT?

Of course, it wasn't all doom and gloom, whatever Charles Dickens tells you. There were some cheery moments, too... weren't there?

I command the waves, go back, go back!

Then the sea came in and wet his royal tootsies. But old King Cnut was no chump, even way back then in 1016. He knew all the time that no king was all-powerful, and his little seaside demonstration proved the point to a lot of silly people.

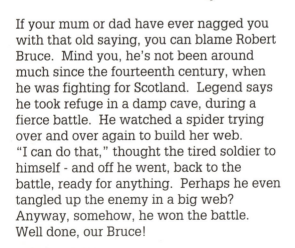

If at first you don't succeed, try and try again.

If your mum or dad have ever nagged you with that old saying, you can blame Robert Bruce. Mind you, he's not been around much since the fourteenth century, when he was fighting for Scotland. Legend says he took refuge in a damp cave, during a fierce battle. He watched a spider trying over and over again to build her web. "I can do that," thought the tired soldier to himself - and off he went, back to the battle, ready for anything. Perhaps he even tangled up the enemy in a big web? Anyway, somehow, he won the battle. Well done, our Bruce!

Over to France, in 1789. Most people there were poor and some were starving. Inside a very grand palace in Paris, the King's wife Marie Antoinette didn't understand why the people were rioting outside her windows. She was told they had no bread. **"Humph, let them eat cake, then!"** she replied, which was a pretty silly thing to say. So silly, that the peasants locked up the King and Queen and later cut off both their heads. So she never said anything silly ever again!

OH DEAR, START AGAIN

Throughout the ages there have been many puzzling discoveries that have made people think again about the World and the Universe...for example:

- Sir Isaac Newton discovered the laws of gravity when an apple fell on his head - who threw the apple?

- The Chinese invented the first clock - how did they know what time to set it to?

- Alexander Graham Bell invented the first telephone - who did he ring?

- Commander Robert Neary discovered the North Pole in 1909 - who put the pole there?

- James Watt invented the steam hammer - why did he want to hammer steam?

- Charles Darwin showed that we are all descended from the same ancestors - why do we speak different languages?

- James Hargreaves invented the 'Spinning Jenny' in 1764 - who was she?

- Catapults have been around for thousands of years - where did they get the elastic?

- Isambard Kingdom Brunel designed many famous bridges and railways - how did he get such a silly name?

- J.K. Starley invented the safety bicycle in 1885 - why don't they fall over going round corners?

JUST LAST WEEK

If history was represented by the life of a single person, then from 1900 until now would be just last week - but what a lot of changes! The most important things that have happened are:

World War One - this was called 'the war to end all wars' but it didn't work.

World War Two - this is the one where your granny and grandad had an argument with someone called Jerry.

The Beatles - four insects called John, Paul, George and Ringo who made girls jump on tables and scream "Aagh...it's the Beatles!".

Fast Food - all right if you can catch it.

Television - the answer to the world's food problems as it grows infinite numbers of couch potatoes.

Superman - why is he never there when you need him?

Star Wars - a big argument between Tom Cruise and Arnold Schwarzenegger.

Computers - the scientific way of avoiding dreary homework.

Suspended Animation - an unfinished film from the Walt Disney studios.

Shell Suits - tidy homes for snails.

Space Travel - the opposite of public transport during the rush hour.

Higher Education - any school more than six hundred metres above sea level.

SO WHAT?

So what will historians tell us in the future? Here are a few headlines from the year 2090 that might give you some clues...

INFLATION Packet of crisps now worth £23.50

Original copy of Survive at School sells for £10,000 at auction to Japanese collector

Giant chicken eggs explode in factory - emergency team scrambled

Package holidays on the Costa Del Saturn very popular this year

ANOTHER TELEPORTER ACCIDENT - survivors say they haven't a leg to stand on

MACAULEY CULKIN MAKES NEW FILM AT AGE 106 - 'Home Alone Yet Again' to be released soon

Robots suffering from metal fatigue go on strike

"Global warming under control" says government official holidaying at the Club Tropicana, North Pole

TIME TRAVELLER VISITS QUEEN VICTORIA - she is not amused

LITTLE GREEN MEN FROM QUORK BRING BACK DINOSAURS "It's monstrous," says spokesperson

...you don't know what history will bring 'til it happens - why not go and make some today?